EXTREME NATURE

DEEP SPACE EXTREMES

JAMES BOW

Crabtree Publishing Company

www.crabtreebooks.com

Crabtree Publishing Company

www.crabtreebooks.com

Author: James Bow

Editor: Molly Aloian

Proofreaders: Adrianna Morganelli, Katherine Berti

Project coordinator: Robert Walker

Production coordinator: Margaret Amy Salter

Prepress technician: Samara Parent

Project editor: Tom Jackson

Designer: Lynne Lennon

Picture researchers: Sophie Mortimer, Sean Hannaway

Managing editor: Tim Harris

Art director: Jeni Child

Design manager: David Poole

Editorial director: Lindsey Lowe

Children's publisher: Anne O'Daly

Photographs:
Ball Aerospace & Technologies Corp: page 24 (top)
Corbis: Reuters: pages 4, 13 (bottom), 20 (bottom);
   Bettmann: page 9 (right); EPA: page 28
NASA: front cover, pages 17 (bottom), 18; HSF:
   pages 5, 10 (bottom), 11 (left), 14-15; JSC: pages 7 (top),
   12, 19 (top), 20 (top), 21 (top); SOHO: page 7 (bottom);
   MSFC: pages 9 (left), 11 (right), 13 (top), 15 (top), 22;
   KSC: pages 10 (top), 29 (top); ESA: page 21 (bottom);
   JPL: pages 23 (top), 25 (right), 26 (center right), 26-27,
   29 (bottom)
Science Photo Library: Christian Darkin: page 23 (bottom)
Shutterstock: Sander Van Sinttruye: pages 4-5; Iofoto:
   pages 6-7; M. Norris: page 17 (top); Alexander Chelmodeev:
   pages 22-23; Jonathan Larsen: pages 24-25; Andrea Danti:
   page 27
Topfoto: page 8
U.S. Air Force: page 15 (bottom)

Illustrations:
BRG: pages 16, 19 (bottom)

Every effort has been made to trace the owners of
copyrighted material.

Library and Archives Canada Cataloguing in Publication

Bow, James, 1972-
   Deep space extremes / James Bow.

(Extreme nature)
Includes index.
ISBN 978-0-7787-4505-1 (bound).--ISBN 978-0-7787-4522-8 (pbk.)

   1. Space environment--Juvenile literature. 2. Deep space--Juvenile
literature. 3. Outer space--Exploration--Juvenile literature. I. Title.
II. Series: Extreme nature (St. Catharines, Ont.)

QB500.22.B69 2008   j629.4'16   C2008-907337-1

Library of Congress Cataloging-in-Publication Data

Bow, James.

   Deep space extremes / James Bow.
      p. cm. -- (Extreme nature)

   Includes index.
   ISBN 978-0-7787-4522-8 (pbk. : alk. paper) -- ISBN 978-0-7787-4505-1
(reinforced library binding : alk. paper)
   1. Space environment--Juvenile literature. 2. Outer space--Exploration--
Juvenile literature. 3. Deep space--Juvenile literature. I. Title. II. Series.

   QB505.B69 2009
   919.904--dc22

                                              2008048643

Crabtree Publishing Company

www.crabtreebooks.com   1-800-387-7650

Published in Canada
Crabtree Publishing
616 Welland Ave.
St. Catharines, Ontario
L2M 5V6

Published in the United States
Crabtree Publishing
PMB16A
350 Fifth Ave., Suite 3308
New York, NY 10118

CONTENTS

INTRODUCTION

People have studied the stars for thousands of years. Thanks to their work, we know that our planet is just one of several planets moving around the Sun. The Sun is just one of billions in our **galaxy**, and there are many millions of galaxies in the universe. Welcome to space!

HIGH FLYER?

Legend has it that 500 years ago in China, a man named Wan-Hu tried to fly to the stars. He attached 47 rockets to a chair. When his assistants lit the rockets, there was a tremendous roar and a great cloud of smoke, and Wan-Hu was never seen again!

▶ Rockets were invented in China about 1,000 years ago. They were fueled by gunpowder, and worked just like today's fireworks.

DEADLY JOURNEY

Even if Wan-Hu made it to space alive, he would not have lived for long. Most of Earth's air is near the surface, so as Wan-Hu flew upward he had less and less air to breathe. Above about 30,000 feet (9,144 m) Wan-Hu would have passed out from lack of oxygen. Wan-Hu would pass the **ozone layer** at about 19 miles (30 km) up. The Sun's **ultraviolet** rays would begin to burn his skin.

EMPTY NOTHINGNESS

Wan-Hu would be dead by the time he got 62 miles (100 km) high. This is where the **atmosphere** ends and the **vacuum** of space begins. It is still too low for Wan-Hu's chair to go into **orbit**, but anyone sitting in it would see Earth curving below and the dark of space above.

▼ *The night sky is a crowded place. The Milky Way is a cloudy strip of light that stretches across the sky. It is made up of many billions of stars.*

FLOAT AND FALL

We do not feel heavy when we are falling. When astronauts are in orbit, they are weightless because they are actually falling, too. Imagine a roller coaster curving right around Earth. An orbiting spacecraft is like a roller-coaster car running along the track, falling in a circle all the way around the planet. It never lands because Earth is always curving away.

THE BLUE PLANET

Earth gives us everything we need to live. There is air to breathe and water to drink. Earth is the only planet with liquid water on its surface. Without water, life as we know it would be impossible.

NEAR NEIGHBOR

Earth is a water planet because our atmosphere keeps us at just the right **temperature**. Even the most extreme weather on Earth—up to 136 °F (58 °C) in the Sahara Desert and down to -128 °F (-89 °C) in Antarctica—is nothing compared to the conditions found elsewhere in space. The surface of Mercury, the planet closest to the Sun, hits a daytime high of 752 °F (400 °C). That is hot enough to melt lead! The temperature on Mercury falls to −392 °F (−235 °C) at night.

EXTREME CONDITIONS

The Sun's surface is about 9,930 °F (5,500 °C), but far out into deep space the temperature is much lower. There, it is almost -464 °F (-276 °C) —or absolute zero. This is the lowest possible temperature. Nothing ever gets colder than this.

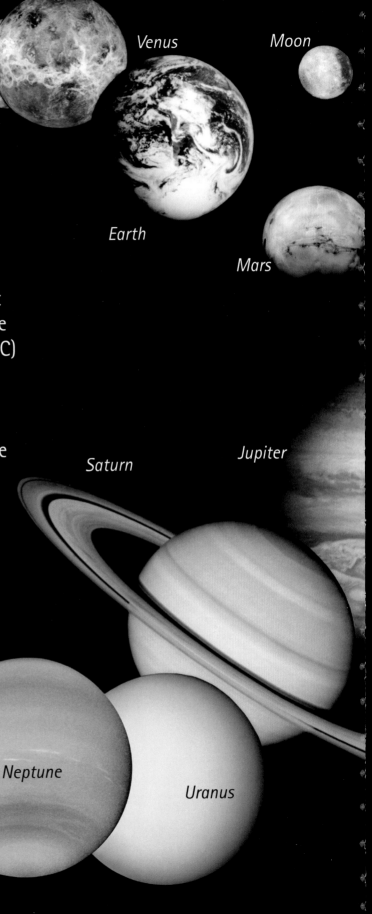

Mercury

Venus

Moon

Earth

Mars

Jupiter

Saturn

Neptune

Uranus

◀ *There are eight planets orbiting the Sun. Earth is the third one out. The planets nearer to the Sun are too hot for life, and the ones further away are too cold and dark.*

In the Extreme

Space is always silent. The sounds we hear on Earth are waves carried in the air, water, and even the ground. However, there are none of these things in space, so there is nothing to carry the sound and no waves for our ears to pick up. Even if you were an astronaut watching a planet explode, you would not hear a thing!

KILLER RAYS

The Sun is a giant fusion reactor. Deep inside, huge forces push tiny particles together into larger ones. This is what happens inside nuclear bombs, only the Sun is billions of times more powerful. The process makes the Sun's heat and light. It also makes dangerous **radiation**. Radiation would kill us if it was not blocked by Earth's atmosphere and **magnetic field**. A spacesuit shields an astronaut from the dangerous radiation.

SURVIVING IN SPACE

One of the first Earthlings to go into space was a dog called Laika. She was a stray from the streets of Moscow, Russia, and was chosen to be the passenger aboard the **Soviet Union's** *Sputnik 2,* an early spacecraft launched in November, 1957.

LAUNCH CHECK

Laika was fitted with sensors to record her body's reaction to space. The shaking during the launch made her breathe four times faster than normal, and her heart rate was double the normal speed. However, Laika made it into space alive!

In the Extreme

Laika was not the very first life form in space. The United States sent flies and corn seeds into space using a German V2 rocket (*left*) in 1947, to test the effects of radiation. In 1949, another V2 rocket carried a rhesus monkey called Albert into space. He was fine throughout the trip but died on his return to Earth, when his pod's parachute failed.

LIFE AND DEATH IN SPACE

After three hours of weightlessness, Laika's body returned to normal. She began to eat her food. This proved that animals, including humans, could survive being launched into space and could cope with being weightless. Sadly, Laika died after seven hours in orbit. A rip in the shield around her cabin meant the air inside got too hot, killing Laika.

▶ *The first spacecraft to be put into orbit was* Sputnik 1. *It was launched by the Soviet Union in October, 1957. The name* Sputnik *means "fellow traveler" in Russian.*

DOGS FROM SPACE

In 1960, dogs Belka and Strelka (*below*) were sent into space aboard Sputnik 5, and were the first large animals to come back from space alive. In 1961, Nikita Khruschev, the Russian leader, gave one of Strelka's puppies to Caroline, the daughter of the U.S. President, John Kennedy. New generations of Strelka's descendants are still thriving today.

⭐ Ham the Chimp was sent into space by **NASA** in 1961.

⭐ Ham wore a little space suit (*right*) and sat inside a capsule. He was trained to work a lever in space so scientists on Earth could check the effects of weightlessness on his brain.

⭐ His capsule landed in the ocean, and Ham lived until 1983.

▼ *An astronaut with a turnip plant growing in space. On Earth, the leaves form a ring around the stem; in space, they grow in all directions.*

WHICH WAY IS UP?

All living things are used to Earth's **gravity**—it is always there, pulling them back down to the ground. When life forms travel into space, the pull of gravity stops having any effect. Living things do not know which way is up and get confused. For example, there is no gravity to tell plants which direction to grow. Instead, roots and leaves grow in wild patterns.

WASTING AWAY

Animal bodies—including human bodies—are always working against gravity. Our hearts pump blood up into our heads—gravity pulls it down again. In the first few days in space, your face feels puffy—the blood does not drain out of it easily. Our muscles are always holding the body upright, so it does not fall over. In weightless conditions, the heart and muscles stop working so hard—but that is not a good thing. Muscles that do not get used get weaker. Bones also get thinner.

In the Extreme

Can spiders spin webs without gravity? In 1973, two garden spiders, Arabella and Anita, were sent into space to build webs. On Earth, a spider uses gravity to lower itself on a thread of silk to make a Y-shaped frame for its web. The space spiders could not do this so their thin webs (*below*) were very wonky.

◄ *An astronaut runs on a treadmill to keep his body strong while in space. He is strapped to the exercise machine so he does not float away when he tries to run.*

COUNTDOWN

IN MOVIES, people sometimes explode if they fall into the vacuum of space without a protective suit. In real life, things are more complicated. A vacuum will kill you—but not instantly. Without any air **pressure**, the saliva in your mouth and the tears in your eyes boil away. Small blood vessels burst, giving you bloodshot eyes and a bloody nose. After ten seconds, your skin starts to swell as your blood boils inside your body. This happens first in the blood vessels near the surface. The effect of the vacuum spreads quickly through the body. In little more than a minute, the blood has expanded so much that your heart bursts. Nevertheless, some astronauts have survived leaks in their space suits and been rescued with only small injuries.

ONE-WAY TRIP?

Even if an astronaut exercises, he or she will be very weak after a long voyage in space. Some experts have suggested that if someone stayed in space for too long, the gravity on Earth might kill them when they returned home.

▶ *Astronaut Ed White was the first American to take a "space walk"—climb out of his spacecraft and float in space. He was kept alive by a pressurized suit.*

WEIGHING THE PROBLEM

Scientists are still figuring out the long-term effects of weightlessness. The longest any human has been in space is 438 days. This record was set by Russian **cosmonaut** Valery Polyakov in 1995.

IN A SPIN

Spaceships could be designed to create a substitute for gravity. If a spacecraft spun around, it would produce a force that pushes the people inside to the floor, a bit like gravity. If we ever set up towns in orbit, it will probably be in huge spinning spacecraft.

In the Extreme

According to the *Guinness Book of World Records*, the "World's Toughest Bacterium" is *Deinococcus radiodurans* (*left*). The bacterium is an extremophile, the scientific name for creatures that survive in extreme environments. This bacteria can even survive in the vacuum of space. It can cope with high radiation. On Earth, it eats nuclear waste! Some people think that extremophiles were the earliest life on our planet and might even have been brought to Earth from outer space by comets.

◀ *Cosmonauts rest after arriving back on Earth. They cannot stand up on their own.*

HUMAN SPACE FLIGHT

Lunar lander

The *V2* was a rocket built by the Germans during World War II. It was built to carry bombs across the world—and was the first rocket to fly into space. After the war, the United States and the Soviet Union competed to be the best at exploring space. The competition became known as the Space Race.

Lunar rover

LEADING THE WAY

The Soviet Union took the lead. They launched the first satellite in 1957. In 1961, Russian Yuri Gagarin became the first man in space. Valentina Tereshkova followed in 1963 as the first woman. In 1966, the uncrewed *Luna 9* was the first

CATCHING UP

The U.S. space program took longer to get going. The first American in space was Alan Shepard who got there a month after Gagarin. The first American woman in space was Sally Ride in 1983. The United States then decided to overtake the Soviets

SMALL STEPS

In 1969, Neil Armstrong became the first person to walk on the Moon. In total, 12 Americans have explored the Moon. The Soviet Union has not sent anyone. The last man visited the Moon in 1972, but there are now plans to go back.

▼ *Astronaut John Young jumps up while exploring the Moon in 1970.*

Vital Statistics

✳ The Saturn V rocket took people to the Moon.

✳ It was 361 feet (110 m) high but only 33 feet (10 m) wide.

✳ It fired in three stages, and could lift 130 tons (118 tonnes) into orbit.

✳ The Saturn V rocket is still the most powerful and noisiest rocket ever to fly.

THE FIRST ASTRONAUT?

In 1960, Joseph Kittinger braved temperatures of -110 °F (-78 °C) to go to the edge of space in a helium balloon. He could not use the balloon to go back down—so he jumped out (*left*). Kittinger parachuted from 102,800 feet (31,300 m). He fell for four minutes and dropped so fast that his body broke the sound barrier.

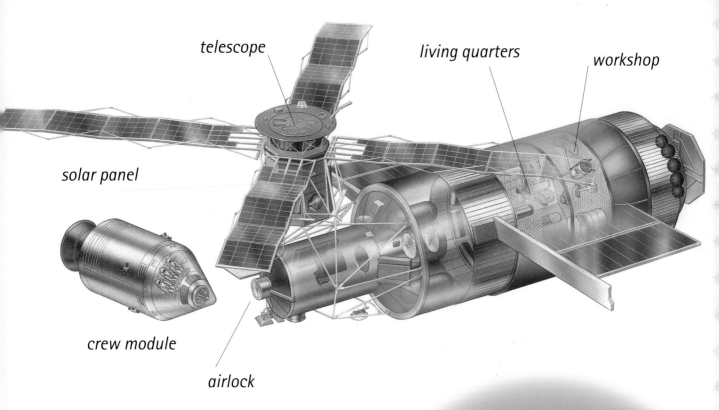

telescope

living quarters

workshop

solar panel

crew module

airlock

▲ Skylab *was the first NASA space station.*
Crews arrived aboard the same type of
spacecraft used to fly to the Moon.

STATIONED IN SPACE

Space flight is very expensive—going
to the Moon cost five percent of
all the money in the United States.
In the 1970s, space scientists began
to look for less expensive ways of
exploring space. The answer was a
space station. The first one was
Salyut 1, launched by the Soviet
Union in 1971. Its first crew lived
onboard for 23 days, but the crew
died on their way back to Earth.
The Soviets launched several more
stations over the next 15 years.

FAST FACTS

★ Weightless astronauts must
strap themselves to toilets when
they go to the bathroom.

★ The toilet has no flush but uses
a vacuum to suck up the waste.

★ Astronauts wash with a damp
cloth (*right*) and suck up the water
with a nozzle. If they take a shower,
they must wear a breathing mask so
they do not choke on droplets.

LAB WORK

Space exploration has given us a lot of technology that helps us here on Earth. Our weather forecasts are only possible thanks to satellites taking measurements of the atmosphere. Space technology used in homes includes water purification systems, scratch-resistant plastic lenses, and liquefied baby food. The thick coats and pants worn by firefighters (*right*) were first used in space.

LAB IN THE SKY

NASA launched a space station called *Skylab* in 1973. The space station was built inside the upper section of a Saturn V space rocket. Instead of flying to the Moon, the rocket only went as far as an orbit around Earth. *Skylab* stayed in orbit for six years. In that time, three crews of astronauts lived aboard the station for a total of 171 days. The station allowed NASA to perform scientific and medical experiments. The crew also made discoveries about the Sun.

SPACE PLANES

Huge space rockets can only be used once. It is impossible to bring them back from space. As they fall back into the atmosphere, **friction** makes the rockets so hot that they burn up. The answer to this problem was the space shuttle. This spacecraft launches like a rocket but comes back to Earth like an airplane, landing on a runway. The shuttle is protected by a heat shield so it can be used again.

INTERNATIONAL MISSION

The Soviet Union focused on a permanent settlement in space. Their most successful space station was *Mir*, which was launched in 1986. It orbited Earth until 2001. It was replaced by the International Space Station (*right*), which is still being built—in space—today.

Vital Statistics

★ The International Space Station (ISS) travels at 17,212 miles per hour (27,700 km/h). It orbits Earth 16 times a day.

★ The ISS is run by the United States, Russia, Japan, Canada, and the European Union. When finished, it will have cost $100 billion, making it the most expensive object ever built.

★ The space station is made up of several modules, or sections. The first two were connected in orbit in 1998. The first crews arrived in 2000.

★ The ISS can be seen from Earth without a telescope. It is due to be finished in 2017.

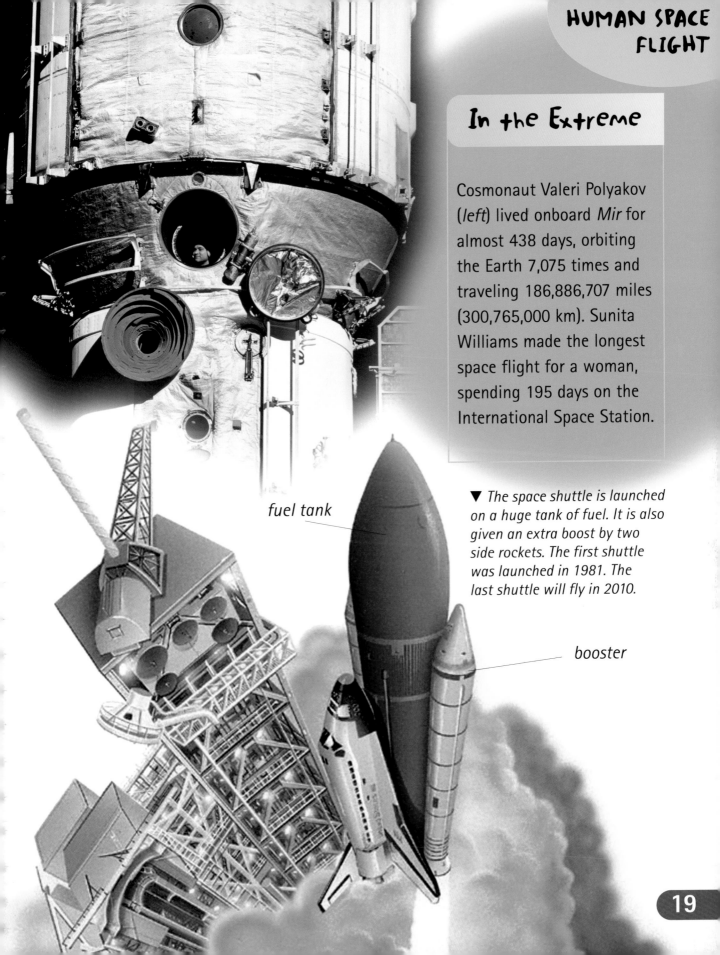

In the Extreme

Cosmonaut Valeri Polyakov (*left*) lived onboard *Mir* for almost 438 days, orbiting the Earth 7,075 times and traveling 186,886,707 miles (300,765,000 km). Sunita Williams made the longest space flight for a woman, spending 195 days on the International Space Station.

fuel tank

▼ *The space shuttle is launched on a huge tank of fuel. It is also given an extra boost by two side rockets. The first shuttle was launched in 1981. The last shuttle will fly in 2010.*

booster

▼ *The Orion spacecraft will have room for four crew members. It will be powered by solar panels.*

MORE MISSIONS

It has been almost 40 years since people last walked on the Moon. However, several countries, including Russia, China, and the United States, have announced plans to send crews back to the Moon. The NASA program is called Constellation. It aims to put astronauts on the Moon in 2020. The Constellation project will then set up the Lunar Refuge—a Moon base. If the Constellation missions are a success then its spacecraft and Moon-base technology could be used to take crew on the even longer flight to Mars.

WANT A HOLIDAY IN SPACE?

American businessman Dennis Tito became the first "space tourist" in 2001 when he visited the International Space Station for ten days. Tito (*right*) paid $20 million for the vacation. Virgin Galactic hopes to take passengers into space by 2010. Each ticket will cost $200,000.

◀ *A permanent Moon base could be set up this century.*

THE DISTANCE PROBLEM

It takes three days to fly to the Moon. A trip to Mars and back would last three years. Voyages to deep space would take much longer. The crew would die in space. Perhaps their grandchildren could be the first humans to orbit a distant star.

SPACE CONSTRUCTION

Constellation will use the same technology used to launch Saturn V rockets and space shuttles. Getting off Earth will still be difficult. A spaceship large enough to explore the **solar system** would be almost impossible to launch into space. If people can learn to live in orbit or on the Moon, we might be able to build these giant spaceships away from Earth. Rocket motors are fueled by hydrogen and oxygen, which are also the ingredients of water. If we can find a source of water on the Moon, we could use that to make rocket fuel for voyages to the planets and beyond.

FAST FACTS

✴ It takes four years for light to reach us from the nearest star, Alpha Centauri. It would take 30,000 years for a spacecraft to reach this star.

✴ The furthest stars we can see (*below*) are 13 billion light years away. It has taken 13 billion years for the light from these stars to reach us.

ALIEN LIFE

Astronomers have wondered about life on other planets almost as soon as they discovered that Earth was just one planet among many others. In 1877, Italian astronomer Giovanni Schiaparelli was sure he saw a canal network on Mars. Thousands of people report seeing UFOs—Unidentified Flying Objects—every year. Are they really alien spaceships?

IS THERE ANYBODY THERE?

As far as we know we are alone in the universe. Uncrewed space probes have told us that Mars and Venus are dead. Scientists are now looking for Earth-like planets outside the solar system. So far they have found nothing.

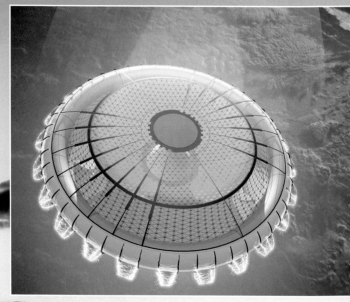

▲ *Alien spaceships are often reported as "flying saucers."*

WHAT ARE THE CHANCES?

If life is possible on Earth, how likely is it that life also exists on distant planets similar to our own? Life is probably very uncommon, but it is likely to be out there somewhere. Experts suggest that the chance of an advanced **civilization** like ours developing in a solar system is one in a billion. There are at least 100 billion solar systems in our **galaxy** alone, so 100 planets could be civilized. The question is, how do we find them?

TROPICAL PARADISE?

The planet Venus is similar in size to Earth. People used to imagine it was a steamy jungle world—after all, Venus is closer to the Sun, so it should be warmer. The first probes to land there discovered that the planet is very hot indeed—so hot that the probes began to melt! The thick clouds produce **acid rain**, and the air pressure on Venus is 92 times more than Earth's. That is enough to crush a human body. The mountains on the barren planet (*left*) have snow made from metal!

WHAT IS ASTROBIOLOGY?

People who look for life on other planets are called astrobiologists. They can only guess at what alien life might be like. They combine what they know about life on Earth to come up with ways that life might have evolved on other worlds. Perhaps we will find jellyfish living around volcanoes in alien oceans (*left*).

DISTANT PLANETS

Astronomers discovered the first **exoplanet** in 1992. Since then, hundreds more have been found. We cannot see the planets themselves, even with the most powerful telescopes. We know that they are there using two main techniques. We can measure the way the star wobbles slightly as its planets orbit around it. We also look for stars that change in brightness. These changes show us that planets are moving in front of the star, blocking out some of its light.

LONG-DISTANCE CALLS

If we do find **extraterrestrial** life that is as intelligent as us, it will not be easy to communicate with them because of the huge distances involved. Even if there were aliens on Alpha Centauri to talk to, we would still have to wait eight years for the Centaurons to reply to our e-mails.

MESSAGE FROM THE STARS

Scientists are also listening for signs of life. Most of this work is done by SETI—the Search for Extraterrestrial Intelligence. SETI began in 1960, when astronomer Frank Drake trained a **radio telescope** at the stars Tau Ceti and Epsilon Eridani. He was searching for radio signals that might have come from an alien civilization. But in almost 50 years of listening, nothing definite has been heard.

JUST RIGHT

Earth moves around the Sun in the Goldilocks orbit—it is not too hot or too cold, like the porridge in the *Three Bears* story. Earth is just far enough from the Sun that the oceans do not boil, but just close enough that we do not become a ball of ice. Scientists are looking for other planets in their own Goldilocks orbits. A few planets have been found in the right place, but they are all balls of gas, not rock like Earth.

◀ *The Very Large Array (VLA) is a radio telescope in New Mexico. It has 27 huge dishes that pick up radio waves from deep space. The VLA has been listening for signals from extraterrestrials for 30 years.*

RARE OR HIDDEN?

Why are aliens so hard to find? Scientists have a number of ideas. Some say deadly bursts of radiation from dying stars could kill all life in large sections of the universe. Others suggest that the steps needed for intelligent life to evolve are so complicated that civilizations are very rare—perhaps we are the only one. Or maybe aliens are everywhere, but we have not figured out how to see them.

ICE MOON

Jupiter's sixth moon, Europa, is covered in a layer of water 62 miles (100 km) thick. The upper layers have frozen solid, but there may be a liquid ocean beneath. Liquid water makes life possible, and astrobiologists think Europa (*below*) is the best place to look for aliens. A submarine probe is planned to visit the moon.

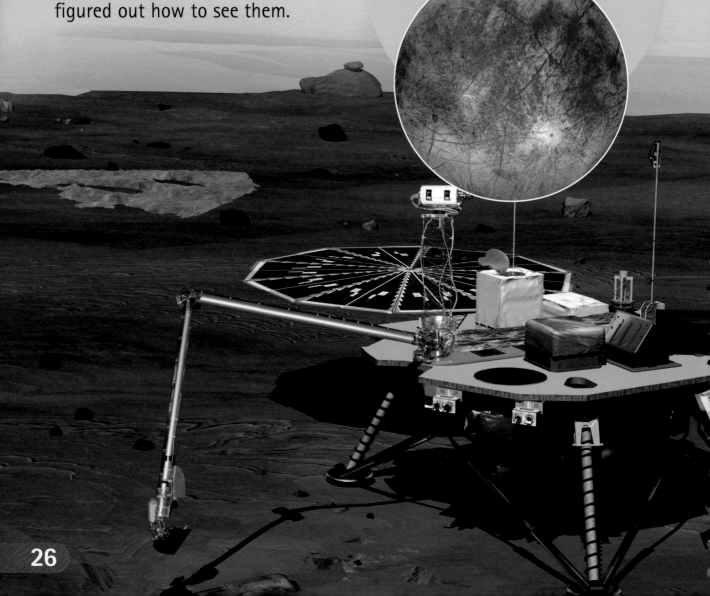

In the Extreme

Did life on Earth come from the stars? Life is based on several complex chemicals, such as DNA and proteins. People have suggested that comets (*right*) made from ice and dust brought these chemicals to Earth billions of years ago. Some bacteria and viruses can survive in space. Perhaps they came from space, too?

◀ *The Phoenix lander is digging into the soil on Mars in search of ice. The lander will also check the ice for chemicals left by life forms that might have lived on Mars in the past.*

LOOKING FOR LIFE

If life is common around the universe, it might have started in other parts of the solar system. Even if this alien life has died out now, we might be able to find remains of it. Mars gets the most attention. The Martian atmosphere contains **methane** gas, which can only last for a few hundred years in the conditions there. Where did it come from? On Earth, methane is made by bacteria in the soil. Is something similar living on Mars?

EXTREME FACTS

SPACE WALKING

EVA, short for Extra-Vehicular Activity, is the official name for "space walks." Cosmonaut Alexey Leonov took the first space walk in 1965. While he was outside the spacecraft, Leonov's spacesuit over-inflated. He could not fit back through the **airlock**. He had to depressurize his suit before climbing back onboard.

TAIKONAUTS

In 2003, China became the third country to put a person into orbit. Yang Liwei (*right*) spent 21 hours aboard *Shenzhou 5* and returned safely. He became the first "Taikonaut," the Chinese word for "astronaut." The name comes from *taikong*, the Chinese word for space. Taikonauts made a space walk in 2008, and China hopes to have a space station by 2010, a Moon landing by 2020, and a crewed probe to Mars by 2060.

CROWDED HOUSE

The largest number of people in one spacecraft at the same time is 13 when the space shuttle *Atlantis* visited the Russian space station *Mir*.

新闻背景
首次载人航天工程的七大系统

FLOATING FREE

Stephen Hawking is a famous English astronomer. In 2007, he was the first quadraplegic (a person with paralyzed arms and legs) to be weightless in the Vomit Comet (*left*). He is now planning to visit space itself.

DROPPING FROM THE SKY

Space agencies use airplanes to train astronauts to work in weightlessness. The aircraft can create weightlessness without leaving Earth's atmosphere. It climbs steeply to several miles above the ground, and then the pilots make the aircraft dive straight down toward the ground again. The plane falls 1.6 miles (2.7 km) in about 20 seconds. As the plane falls, so do the passengers inside. They experience weightlessness during the fall. Most people get sick on the flight, which earns the plane its nickname the "Vomit Comet."

SOUNDS OF EARTH

Voyager I is a 1970s space probe that has now left the solar system. If one day aliens find it, they can listen to the sounds of Earth recorded on a gold disk (*right*). There are also instructions on how to find Earth.

GROWING IN SPACE

A system of growing plants without soil was developed in space. Plant roots usually get their water from the ground. The roots of "aeroponic" plants are sprayed with water that also contains the chemicals they need. Perhaps one day space stations will have greenhouses.

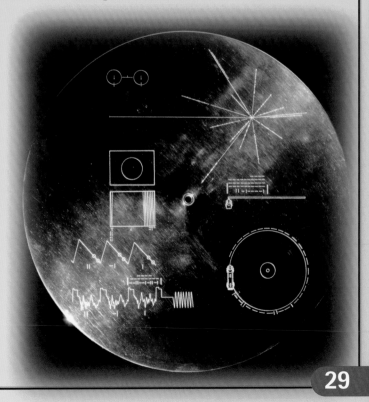

GLOSSARY

acid rain Rain that contains chemicals that eat away at solid substances

airlock The door system that lets people move between space and an air-filled cabin without letting the air out

astronaut The American name for a traveler in space

atmosphere The gases around Earth

civilizations Organized societies

cosmosnaut The Russian name for a space traveler

exoplanet A planet that goes around another star in another solar system

extraterrestrial An alien

friction The drag force that is created when things rub together

galaxy A large group of stars. Our galaxy is called the Milky Way

gravity The force that pulls us down to Earth

magnetic field The region of space in which a magnet's force works

methane A natural gas used as fuel

NASA The U.S. space agency

orbit The circular route one object takes around another in space

ozone layer A protective gas in the atmosphere

pressure How much air or water pushes down on an object

radiation Rays such as light and heat

radio telescope A machine that makes images using radio waves instead of light

solar system The system of planets and moons that orbits the Sun

Soviet Union A large empire ruled by Russia in the 20th century

temperature A measure of how hot or cold something is

ultraviolet Invisible light from the Sun that causes sunburn

vacuum An area that has nothing in it, not even gas

weightless To float in the air and not be pulled down to the ground by gravity, and therefore have no weight at all

FURTHER RESOURCES

BOOKS

Can We Travel to the Stars?: Space Flight and Space Exploration by Andrew Solway. Chicago, IL: Heinemann Library, 2006.

Disasters in Space Exploration by Gregory L. Vogt. Brookfield, CT: Millbrook Press, 2003.

Space and Flight Experiments by Louis V. Loeschnig and Dave Garbot. New York, NY: Sterling Publishing Company, 2006.

Space Travel by Patricia Whitehouse. Chicago, IL: Heinemann Library, 2004.

WEBSITES

NASA's Students Page

http://www.nasa.gov/audience/forstudents/k-4/index.html

National Geographic's Interactive Solar System

http://science.nationalgeographic.com/science/space/solar-system

Interactive Guide to Constellation Moon Program from the Discovery Channel

http://science.discovery.com/tv/space-week/constellation/constellation.html

How Space Food Works

http://science.howstuffworks.com/space-food.htm

INDEX

Printed in the U.S.A. — BG